100 QUESTIONS

YOU'D NEVER ASK YOUR PARENTS

Elisabeth Henderson & Nancy Armstrong, M.D.

100 QUESTIONS

REVISED EDITION

YOU'D NEVER ASK YOUR PARENTS

Straight Answers to Teens' Questions About Sex, Sexuality, and Health

ROARING BROOK PRESS  NEW YORK

Copyright © 2007, 2013 by Elisabeth Henderson

Published by Roaring Brook Press

Roaring Brook Press is a division of Holtzbrinck Publishing Holdings Limited Partnership

175 Fifth Avenue, New York, New York 10010

Originally published in 2007 by Uppman Publishing, a division of Colevan International, LLC, Richmond, Virginia.

Library of Congress Cataloging-in-Publication Data

Henderson, Elisabeth.
 100 questions you'd never ask your parents / Elisabeth Henderson & Nancy Armstrong.— 1st ed.
   p. cm.
  ISBN 978-1-59643-869-9 (ebook)—ISBN 978-1-59643-875-0 (hbk.)—
ISBN 978-1-59643-868-2 (pbk.)
 1. Sex instruction for teenagers—Juvenile literature.   2. Sex—Juvenile literature.
 I. Armstrong, Nancy.   II. Title.   III. Title: One hundred questions you'd never ask your parents.
  HQ35.H38 2013
  306.70835—dc23

                                                            2012033760

Roaring Brook Press books may be purchased for business or promotional use. For information on bulk purchases please contact Macmillan Corporate and Premium Sales Department at (800) 221-7945 x5442 or by email at specialmarkets@macmillan.com.

Revised Edition 2013
Printed in the United States of America
Hardcover: 10 9 8 7 6 5 4 3 2 1
Paperback: 10 9 8 7 6 5 4 3 2 1

For Cole and Evan,
in case they never ask

Contents

Foreword

100 Questions originated with teens.

During my years as a middle school teacher, one of my responsibilities was teaching sex education classes. Some of the 100 questions in this book were asked during those classes, while many of them were asked after class. I heard, "Ms. H., may I ask you something after school?" more than once. What was both consistent and obvious about each of these Q&A sessions was that teens wanted factually based, nonjudgmental answers to their important questions. Often, however, they were too embarrassed to ask in front of their peers, or of their family.

Teens were asking, though. Over the years, whether it was my students, children of friends, or even younger family members, all of these questions originated directly from teens. I am very proud that collectively, they inspired this book and are its "original authors." Without the brave teens who asked the hard or "embarrassing" questions, there would be no *100 Questions*.

I tell parents all the time that if they have a child 11 years or older, their child is asking questions. It's just a matter of who they're asking and how reliable the answers are. As a mother, I want to ensure that kids are empowered with knowledge that will help them make safe, informed, educated decisions about the life experiences they inevitably grow into.

Dr. Nancy and I have been overwhelmed with the response to the original *100 Questions*. We couldn't have predicted the incredibly positive feedback from teens, parents trying to figure out how to talk about these subjects with their children, and health workers looking for a resource that is written in a "real" voice.

I'd like to thank all the tweens and teens who asked me these questions and made this book possible.

Note

I am happy with every part of this book except one. I struggled with word choice when referring to girls. I couldn't say "guys and ladies," it is too formal, and "guys and chicks" was too demeaning. There just isn't a good counterpart to "guys." "Girls" seems to go better with "boys" and sounds too young when writing about pregnancy or intercourse. Thus, my disclaimer: I've settled on using "guys and girls," but if you can think of a better wording, I welcome and appreciate your suggestions. Until then, please know that when I write "girls," I am referring to tween and teen young women of pre-pubescent age or above.

100 QUESTIONS

YOU'D NEVER ASK YOUR PARENTS

What does an orgasm feel like?

You've asked one of the most common questions teens have, so be assured you're not alone in wondering.

An orgasm is the emotional and physical sensations that are felt at the end of sexual arousal when built-up muscle tension in the body is released. Put simply, it is the climax of the sensations that have been brought about by sexual excitement. Having an orgasm is also sometimes called "cumming."

If you ask ten people what an orgasm feels like, you might get ten different answers because orgasms are unique to each person. For some people, an orgasm involves the whole body—the heart races, the person may vocalize sounds or words, the muscles throughout the body may twitch, breathing can be heavy, and the person may feel flushed. For others, the feeling is more concentrated and remains in the areas of the vagina or penis. Although an orgasm will feel different to each person, it is a pleasurable feeling and often associated with euphoria and excitement. It has been described as feeling like a very strong tingling, pleasant and pulsating muscle contractions, or a warm throbbing.

When I have sex the first time, will people be able to tell?

No. Although you may feel like everybody knows, they likely won't. You won't look any different, and there will be no outward physical signs that you've had sex. You may, however, feel differently because having sex for the first time is such a big decision, both emotionally and physically. Unless you act differently, however, it is unlikely that anybody will know.

Can a girl get pregnant even if she doesn't orgasm?

Absolutely. A girl can get pregnant whether or not she has an orgasm. That a girl can avoid getting pregnant by not having an orgasm is one of the biggest myths among teens. An orgasm, or lack of one, does not affect whether or not a girl can become pregnant.

What does affect a girl's ability to get pregnant is whether or not she is ovulating. Once a month a girl ovulates, which means her body releases an egg.* If the egg is fertilized with a guy's sperm, it may eventually develop into a baby. The timing of the release of the egg (ovulation) is based upon the girl's menstrual cycle, or period.

Remember, lack of an orgasm has no effect on whether or not an egg is released. So, yes, a girl can get pregnant even if she doesn't orgasm.

*Some girls ovulate more often, some less. Generally speaking, a girl will ovulate once every 28 days.

What is a wet dream?

A wet dream is an erotic dream that ends in orgasm and ejaculation. Wet dreams occur most frequently during a guy's teen and early adult years and are completely involuntary. Some guys wake up as they are ejaculating while others sleep right through it. Wet dreams are common and are no cause for concern; many guys experience them as they go through puberty.

Girls also experience wet dreams, though the percentage of girls who do is lower than the percentage of guys who do. Of the girls who do have wet dreams, many tend to have them less frequently than guys. A girl who has a wet dream will wake up feeling like she just experienced an orgasm, or may wake up in the middle of the orgasm, and will likely have increased wetness or vaginal secretions.

Some guys, and even more girls, never experience wet dreams. Whether you do or don't, wet dreams are a normal part of growing up.

How old do I have to be to buy condoms?

There is no age restriction on buying condoms; a person of any age can buy them. Condoms can be purchased at most grocery stores, drugstores, and convenience stores. A pharmacist can discreetly answer any questions you have about them.

At what age do people usually start having sex?

The answer might be higher than you think. The average age that U.S. teens start having sex is 17, with the majority of high school students not having sex at all (53%).

The age that most teens start having sex and the age that someone is ready to start having sex can be two very different things. Only you can determine the right time for you, and it's an important decision. Question 30 (How will I know when I'm ready to have sex?) may help you decide when it is the right time for you.

7

Am I still a virgin if I use a tampon?

Yes. A virgin is someone who has never had sexual intercourse. Until you do, you're a virgin; using a tampon doesn't change that.

Why does this question get asked so often? Virgin girls often have an intact hymen, which is a very thin and flexible membrane that stretches across the opening of the vagina, partially covering it. Some people mistakenly think that a girl loses her virginity if her hymen breaks. Very occasionally, tampon use can break a girl's hymen. (Masturbation, sports, horseback riding, and other physical activities can also break the hymen.) Using a tampon, even if it were to break the hymen, does not mean a girl isn't a virgin. The only way for a girl to lose her virginity is to have sex.

Can a girl get pregnant if she has sex during her period?

Yes. While it's rare for a girl to get pregnant during her period, she absolutely could. Usually a girl's period occurs about 14 days after she ovulates. However, if she has a short menstrual cycle and long periods, sometimes ovulation (when a girl releases an egg) can overlap with her period. If it does, she would be fertile during her period, and if she had sex, she could get pregnant.

Also keep in mind that bleeding is not always due to a menstrual period. Sometimes girls experience small amounts of bleeding during ovulation, as the egg is released and travels down the fallopian tube. This bleeding can be mistaken for a period, but is actually when a girl is most fertile. Remember, unprotected sex at any time is a risk, even during your period. It is always better to use protection and be safe.

I haven't hit puberty yet. What's wrong with me?

Puberty isn't a science, and going through it is different for everyone. Some people start early, some start late; some go through it quickly and for others it feels like it takes forever. The good news is that all these differences, while a cause of worry for many teens, are completely normal.

There is no exact age when guys and girls start puberty. Generally speaking, however, girls start puberty between the ages 8 and 13 and guys start a little later, between 9 and 14 (although it can be earlier or later for both groups). For teens who start puberty late, waiting can be difficult but it is not a reason to worry. "Late bloomers," as they are sometimes called, are almost always healthy.

The age that a person starts puberty is generally dependent on genetics. A girl who develops later may find out that other people in her family also developed later than usual. There are other factors, however, that can cause a small percentage of teens to have delayed development. These factors include chronic illness, malnourishment, or problems with the pituitary or thyroid glands. If you have concerns, talking to a parent or doctor can be a good way to relieve your worries and ensure that you are developing normally.

10

What's the difference between an orgasm and ejaculation?

People often use the terms "orgasm" and "ejaculation" interchangeably, but they are very different things.

An orgasm is the release of built-up muscle tension in the body that is a result of sexual arousal. Involuntary actions—such as quick cycles of pleasurable muscle spasms, vocalizations, and euphoria—are often associated with having an orgasm. Guys and girls both experience orgasms.

Ejaculation is when semen is ejected from a guy's penis. A guy almost always ejaculates when he has an orgasm. Additionally, a guy could ejaculate without having an orgasm (though this is not common) or have an orgasm without ejaculating. (This can occur in pre-pubescent boys who don't yet produce semen.) Most often, however, orgasm and ejaculation occur together in guys.

What about girls? Do they ejaculate? Girls definitely experience orgasms and all the muscle spasms and pleasurable feelings that are part of them. Many people say they don't ejaculate and that any wetness that is present during sex is just lubrication that the body makes to accommodate the penis going into the vagina. Others say that girls do ejaculate and that when they do, noticeably more clear fluid comes out of the urethra (fluid that is not urine). No explanation has been given for where this fluid comes from, and whether or not girls "ejaculate" is still undetermined.

Do a guy's balls really "drop" during puberty?

Contrary to popular belief, a guy's balls (or testicles or testes) do not "drop" during puberty. They actually descend into the scrotum just before birth, so they are there the entire time.

A guy's testicles grow throughout his childhood, but they begin to grow faster during puberty. As they grow bigger and longer, they look more prominent and hang lower, overall. This is why some people say they "drop" during puberty. Some guys' testicles will grow a lot, while others' will not. There is a wide range of normal sizes—just as guys grow to be many different heights. Also, while a guy's two testicles usually grow to be the same size, it's not uncommon for one to be slightly bigger than the other, or for one to hang slightly lower than the other one.

Can a guy wear a condom during oral sex?

Absolutely, and it is important for both partners that he do so. Sexually transmitted diseases such as hepatitis B, genital warts, syphilis, gonorrhea, HIV,
and herpes can all be spread through oral sex. The best way to reduce the risk
of infection is to reduce your exposure, so be smart and be protected. A guy
should wear a non-lubricated condom when receiving oral sex; the lubrication
that comes on some condoms is not something you'd want to taste or ingest.

Is my penis a normal size?

Every guy has a different-sized penis, and all sizes are normal; there is generally no "abnormal" when it comes to penis size. If one guy's eyes are blue and another guy's are brown, both are "normal," they're just different. It's the same with penises. Even so, penis size is still a big concern for many guys, in part because over the years the size of an average penis has been greatly exaggerated. The true, average length of an erect penis in an adult male is between 5 and 6 inches.

Will condoms protect me from all diseases?

When used correctly, condoms are an important and highly effective barrier to the spread of chlamydia, gonorrhea, hepatitis B, HIV, and other sexually transmitted diseases (STDs). However, condoms are only as good as the people who use them, so they are not foolproof. They can fail due to human error, breakage, and inconsistent or incorrect use.

While condoms are effective in preventing STDs that are transmitted by fluid or skin-to-skin contact, not all areas of contact get covered by a condom. If your partner has open sores that are not covered by the condom (from genital warts, syphilis, or herpes, for example) the diseases can still be spread to you. Additionally, condoms made from sheepskin are inadequate in preventing the spread of HIV and other viruses because they have natural pores that the viruses can pass through.

Thus, while latex condoms are an effective protection against the spread of diseases, there is still a risk any time you have sex.

15

Can I get HIV from kissing? From oral sex?

Medical experts agree that under most circumstances, you can't become infected with HIV through casual kissing. While saliva does contain HIV, it only contains very small concentrations and not enough to transfer the infection. Therefore, casual kissing, such as on the cheek or with a closed mouth, is considered low risk.

While the exchange of saliva alone poses very little risk, if an infected person's saliva has blood in it, there is a definite risk of transmitting HIV. If both partners have cuts or sores on their lips, mouth, or gums (even if they are not readily visible), there is a risk that HIV could be transferred through blood contact. This risk has resulted in the Centers for Disease Control recommending against open-mouth kissing with an infected partner.

Giving or receiving oral sex can result in either partner becoming infected with HIV. So if the person giving oral sex has HIV, it can be transmitted to the receiving person. And if the receiving person has HIV, it can be transmitted to the person performing the oral sex. Although using a condom during oral sex reduces the risk of transferring HIV, having oral sex with an infected partner, even with a condom, poses a real and significant risk.

How can I get free and confidential STD testing?

This is an important question. If you think you may have been exposed to a sexually transmitted disease, it is very important that you be tested, not only for your own health, but also for the health of your partner, or future partners. All states offer testing for sexually transmitted diseases through their Departments of Health. Testing may be confidential but not free, free but not confidential, or free and confidential. In many states, minors do not need parental consent for examination and treatment. To find a clinic in your area, contact your local Department of Health. You may also consider asking your school nurse or your doctor about your options. In either case, be sure to ask if your conversation and testing will be kept confidential before you begin. And be proud of yourself; being tested is a responsible and safe choice.

What's the best birth control?

Deciding what the best birth control is depends on (1) what is safest and most effective, and (2) what you are personally comfortable with. The only sure way to prevent pregnancy and the spread of most STDs is to not have sex at all (abstinence). All other types of birth control reduce the risks, but they are no guarantee.

There are many types of birth control other than abstinence, and each has its own advantages and disadvantages. Remember, however, that birth control is not foolproof, and people who use it can become pregnant if they use it incorrectly or if something goes wrong (like a condom breaking). Also keep in mind that while all birth control methods can help prevent pregnancy, not all of them help prevent the transmission of STDs.

Birth control pills are one of the most popular forms of contraception because they are easy to take and highly effective. If taken every day as directed, the pill has a 99% success rate in preventing pregnancy. It does not, however, offer any protection against STDs. Condoms are also very popular because they are easy to get, inexpensive, and help protect against the spread of STDs. Typically, condoms have an 85% success rate in preventing pregnancy. Another good alternative is to use both the pill and a condom to further reduce the chances of getting an STD or becoming pregnant.

There are many other contraceptives available. You may want to talk to your doctor about what birth control method is best for you.

Does douching after sex prevent pregnancy?

No, this is a widespread myth.

Douching is when a girl squeezes a mixture of water and either a mild soap or vinegar into her vagina to cleanse it.* Douching does not prevent pregnancy. In fact, as the solution is sprayed, it may push the sperm farther up the vagina, actually increasing the chance of pregnancy. Also, sperm are very fast swimmers, so by the time a girl douches, the sperm could have already reached the cervix. As popular as this myth is among teens, it is completely untrue.

*Douches are premixed, store-bought items and should never be made at home.

What are the first signs of puberty?

Puberty is the physical transition of a child into an adult who is capable of reproduction. Girls generally start puberty between the ages 8 and 13, and guys generally start later, between the ages of 9 and 14. It is completely normal, however, for some people to start puberty a little earlier or later.

In girls, the first sign of puberty is usually breast development, sometime around the age of 10 or 11. Six to twelve months later, pubic hair begins to grow and fill in. Around the age of 12 or 13, girls can also expect to start menstruating, or having a period.

In guys, the first sign of puberty is usually the testes, or "balls," getting larger. Next is often penis growth, which continues until a guy is about 18 years old. Soon after the penis starts to grow, pubic hair also begins to grow, followed by body and facial hair over the next few years. A guy will also experience his voice "cracking" as his voice deepens to its final, adult tone.

Both guys and girls will grow taller, and their body shapes will change as they go through puberty. They may also experience body odor and acne during this time.

Remember, it is normal for people to begin developing at different ages and to continue at different rates. If you have any concerns, talking to a parent, counselor, or doctor can be a good way to alleviate and address them.

Does alcohol really kill brain cells?

Research studies disagree about whether alcohol kills brain cells or not. The generally accepted consensus, however, is that while alcohol may not kill brain cells*, it does damage the fibers that carry information between the brain cells, thereby impairing communication between the cells. All studies agree that alcohol has significant and negative effects on the brain, damaging both its structure and its functions.

Some of the damage to the brain is noticeable after one or two drinks and then resolves itself once the drinking stops. Examples of this short-term damage are blurred vision, slurred speech, weakened memory, slow reaction times, and difficulty walking or driving. Other brain damage occurs from heavy, long-term drinking and persists even after a person is sober. This type of brain damage includes shrinkage of the brain as well as trouble with learning, memory, movement, and coordination.

Teens who drink alcohol may interrupt important brain development. This

*Alcohol does kill the brain cells of a developing fetus if a pregnant woman drinks.

can lead to poor mental function (problems with memory, judgment, and language) and worsened academic achievement. So, although whether or not alcohol kills brain cells is still being debated, the negative effects it can have in both the short and long term are clear.

What is pre-ejaculate?

Pre-ejaculate is the clear, slippery, slightly thick fluid that comes out of a penis when a guy is sexually aroused. It is usually secreted (released) during masturbation, foreplay, or any time before a guy ejaculates, or "cums," and is therefore sometimes called "pre-cum." Some guys produce very small amounts, and some guys produce a lot.

Pre-ejaculate serves two purposes. First, it gets the urethra ready for the ejaculation of semen. Second, it lubricates the penis during sexual arousal.

Pre-ejaculate contains enough sperm to get a girl pregnant and, in an infected person, will also contain HIV.

22

My breasts are two different sizes. Is this normal?

Absolutely. It is very common for a girl's breasts to be slightly to moderately different in size. A girl's nipples may be different sizes, too. Nobody's breasts are exactly the same size and this is normal. Some girls may worry that there is a medical problem with their breasts, but in teens this is most likely not the case.

Girls may begin to notice a difference in the size of their breasts during puberty, when the breasts begin to grow, or "bud." One breast may grow more than the other, or faster than the other. In some cases, breast sizes even out and a girl's breast sizes are more similar to each other than they once were. In other cases, they continue to be somewhat different, even when fully developed. Both types of development are normal. If you're concerned, however, talk to your doctor and get reassurance. And if you aren't comfortable with how your breasts look under clothes, you can pad one side of your bra to help even out their appearance.

What is a cold sore?

Cold sores, also known as herpes or fever blisters, are caused by the herpes simplex virus. They look like small blisters that appear on the lips, inside the mouth, and adjacent to the mouth. Cold sores usually persist for 10 to 14 days.

When a cold sore appears, the area will first become tingly and sensitive to touch. A person will be able to feel, but not see, a small hard spot. Usually by day three, tiny blisters have formed. These blisters sometimes fill with fluid before splitting and becoming painful and raw. Eventually, the area will begin to scab over and heal itself.

Cold sores are very common and are contagious. A person with an active cold sore should avoid kissing, sharing a glass or utensils, and touching the cold sore and then touching someone else. He or she should also wash hands regularly to prevent the spread of the herpes virus to other parts of the body, or to someone else. And no matter what, a person with a cold sore should never pick at it. Doing so will slow down the healing process and increase the chance of spreading the virus.

Once someone has been infected with the herpes virus, he or she has it forever; cold sores can't be cured. At random times throughout the person's life, a cold sore may simply recur spontaneously. While this can be aggravating, the good news is that a cold sore's pain, frequency, and duration can be lessened with medication. Over-the-counter medications are available at drugstores, and there are effective prescription medications available through your doctor.

Where can I get confidential answers to my questions about sex?

Confidential counseling about sex and other topics is available to teens through several sources.

Your counselor at school will likely keep your conversation confidential as long as you are not talking about hurting yourself or others. Many doctors will treat their teen patients confidentially, although some require a parent's permission before doing so; ask your doctor about his or her policies. Public health clinics also offer confidential advice about sexual health and other health matters, at reduced rates to teens. If you're not sure whether your conversation with someone will be treated confidentially, ask up front before you discuss details.

It would be an oversight to not mention the Internet, but the Internet has a lot of incorrect information on it, so choose your sources and websites wisely. Rely on information from established organizations or government sources such as the Centers for Disease Control or the National Institutes of Health, as opposed to blogs and smaller websites. Also keep in mind that the pages you visit on the Internet are logged in your computer, so it's not confidential; if someone really wanted to know what you were looking at online, he or she could find out. Besides, with such an important topic, talking to a person would probably be much more beneficial.

25

How much semen is there when a guy ejaculates?

The average amount of semen per ejaculation is one to two teaspoons. This amount varies slightly from one guy to another. It can also vary depending on the amount of time between ejaculations and the guy's level of arousal.

Are depression and being sad the same thing?

Sadness is a natural reaction to painful experiences or situations. It is a healthy way to experience your feelings and adjust to a disappointment, change, or loss. Being sad is part of a healing process people go through, and the feeling usually lasts anywhere from a few hours to a few days. Everybody gets sad sometimes.

Depression is very different from sadness. It is a state of despair that lasts for more than two weeks and is so severe that it disrupts a person's life. The person's social interactions, daily schedule, and activities are impacted because of the extreme unhappiness. People who are depressed may describe "feeling sad for no reason" and can feel unmotivated, irritable, tired, and uncaring about things that were once important to them. Depressed people may also have a noticeable change in appetite, problems sleeping, and trouble concentrating. They often describe feeling like there is no hope. Although it is a serious condition that requires treatment, with help depression can be overcome and a person can live a happy and healthy life. If you feel you are depressed, or experience periodic bouts of depression, reach out to a trusted adult for support. There are many resources that can provide help and relief to you.

What is oral sex?

Oral sex is when a person's mouth or tongue is used to stimulate another person's genitalia, including a guy's penis, a girl's clitoris and vagina, and the anus. When oral sex is performed on a guy it is called fellatio; when it is performed on a girl it is called cunnilingus. Both are sometimes referred to as "going down" on a partner.

Is it normal to get an erection for no reason at all?

Yes, it is completely normal to get an erection for no reason at all. Almost every guy experiences spontaneous erections as he goes through puberty because of the hormonal changes that are occurring in his body.

While it's normal to get spontaneous erections, it doesn't make them any less embarrassing to the person experiencing them. Since they're spontaneous, there's no telling when they may occur—in the middle of class, at sports practice, at dinner—there's just no way to predict. The good news is, the more a guy ignores it and thinks of mundane things, the quicker it will likely end. Until it does, a guy can conceal a spontaneous erection with baggy clothes or by holding something in front of his body, like a book.

Is smoking safe if I don't inhale?

No, smoking is never safe. When you inhale, nicotine enters the bloodstream through the lungs. Even if you don't inhale, nicotine can be absorbed through the lining of the mouth. This can eventually lead to cancer of the mouth, esophagus, larynx, lungs, bladder, or pancreas. It can also lead to sinus disease, emphysema, chronic bronchitis, coronary heart disease, and other diseases. Whether or not you inhale, smoking is harmful to your health and could eventually even result in death.

30

How will I know when I'm ready to have sex?

Having sex for the first time is a huge decision. Asking yourself if you're ready means you already recognize this and are carefully thinking it through.

Everybody is different, and knowing when is right for you is an individual decision. There is no set age or time that defines it. Keep in mind that while you are the only person who will know when you're ready, you may not recognize if you aren't ready. There are people who thought they were ready, but later wished they had waited a while longer. Be sure you are comfortable with your decision before you do anything because you can always have sex later, but you can never go back.

When making your decision, you will have to weigh a lot of important considerations. Some questions you could ask yourself to help you decide if you are ready to have sex or not are:

- Does my decision coincide with my morals, character, and family values?
- Do I know how to get, and properly use, birth control?
- Could I have regrets about my decision later?

- Am I emotionally ready to share myself in such an intimate and important way?
- Can I openly discuss my feelings and concerns with my partner?
- Am I considering having sex because I want to or because I feel pressured to?
- Will I be proud of myself and my decision if people find out about it?
- Am I ready to take responsibility for any possible consequences of my decision, such as disease or pregnancy?

Talking to a parent, other close family member, counselor, or doctor could help you make this very important decision. Although talking about sex might be hard to do, it is easier than regretting the decision you make, no matter which one it is. Get advice from people who love, support, and want the best for you. And be sure before you do anything.

31

Are tampons less safe than pads?

This is a common question girls have. Tampons currently made in the U.S. have been deemed safe by the FDA (Food and Drug Administration), which regulates tampon safety. While there are many myths out there about high levels of dioxin (a chemical), bleach, and asbestos being in tampons, none of these are true. In fact, what you eat may expose you to higher doses of dioxin than tampons.

Tampons and pads are both safe to use. Some girls may further choose to use organic pads and tampons.

What are anorexia and bulimia?

Anorexia and bulimia are both eating disorders. People who have anorexia or bulimia have a distorted body image, meaning they don't see their body as it really is. They generally see themselves as overweight or unattractive, no matter how skinny or attractive they really are. Anorexia and bulimia are also characterized by an obsessive fear of weight gain. They are both psychological conditions wherein people use food to address emotional pain, but they are characterized by physical symptoms.

People who are anorexic eat very little and essentially starve themselves. They may also exercise excessively in order to keep weight off, or use diet pills or laxatives for the same reason. Anorexics maintain a body weight that is at least 15% less than their healthy body weight range. In addition to unhealthy weight loss, anorexia is also very harmful in other ways. Anorexics may experience heart failure, stunted growth, thinning hair, problems with their immune system, changes in brain structure, and even death.

People who are bulimic eat a large amount of food and then purposefully vomit it up. This pattern of excessive, uncontrolled overeating followed by purging is called "binge eating." Bulimics may also purge their body of the food by using laxatives and medications or by exercising excessively. Bulimics sometimes use binge eating as a response to stress, depression, or self-esteem issues. Unlike anorexics, bulimics are often within a normal weight range and appear to be physically healthy. They often, however, experience an irregular heartbeat, heartburn, constipation, weakness, exhaustion, and heart attacks. They also often have cavities, erosion of tooth enamel, a sore throat, abdominal pain, ulcers, rupturing of the stomach, and increased risk of suicidal behaviors. Like anorexia, bulimia is a serious and life-threatening disorder.

Approximately 10% of people with anorexia and bulimia die directly from the diseases or from their harmful effects. The good news is that both anorexia and bulimia are treatable. If you believe you are suffering from anorexia or bulimia, the first step is to talk to someone you trust. Your parents, doctor, school counselor, or a trusted family friend are just a few people you may consider going to. They will help you get the resources and support you'll need to get well and will be glad you've confided in them.

If you're not ready to talk to someone yet, an excellent resource is the ANAD—the National Association of Anorexia Nervosa and Associated Disorders (www.anad.org). You'll find links for treatment and referrals as well as contact information for support groups, which are organized by state. There is also a message board and chat rooms for more information and support. Additionally, almost every city has treatment programs at eating disorder treatment centers. If you need more help finding one, ANAD can help with that, too.

Can a virgin get an STD?

Yes, a virgin can get an STD. Sexually transmitted diseases, or STDs, can be transferred through sexual intercourse as the name suggests, but also through sexual touching. Anytime you have skin-to-skin contact with an infected partner, you are at risk for getting an STD. Diseases such as HPV (also known as human papillomavirus or genital warts), chlamydia, and genital herpes, among other diseases, can all be spread without having sex. So, for example, if a guy has warts on his hand and masturbates his partner, he can spread the infection. Or if a girl has a cold sore and performs oral sex on her partner, she can spread the herpes infection to her partner's genital area. Keep in mind that a person with an STD may not know he or she has one because STDs can lie latent in the body for up to a year before showing any symptoms.

Some STDs can also be passed from a mother to her fetus, either in the uterus or during childbirth. This is another way a virgin could have an STD.

How do I bring up using a condom with my partner?

Talking about how to have safer sex with your partner is very important. While it might be embarrassing at first, it is absolutely necessary if you're going to share in the intimacy and responsibility of sex. One of the easiest ways to bring it up is to just take a deep breath, be direct, and say what you feel. Highlight the importance of protecting yourselves against diseases. (Remember, it is possible that one of you may already have an STD, even if you haven't seen any symptoms of it yet.) Discuss the importance of protecting against an unplanned pregnancy. Talk about the responsibilities that would arise if you didn't use a condom and you either spread an infection to your partner, or pregnancy occurred.

Using a condom will help protect both you and your partner. Bringing up the topic of using a condom may be a little awkward at first, but you and your partner will both be glad you did.

Does the first time hurt?

For a guy, the first time he has sex with a girl should not hurt. It may be a nervous time, but it should not be a painful time. If it is painful, something could be wrong and he may want to visit his doctor and get checked out.

A guy who has sex with another guy may experience anything from pleasure to pain the first time. A common cause of discomfort is a lack of adequate lubrication. Use of an artificial lubricant will help prevent friction pain for both partners, both the first time and subsequent times. Also, ensuring the receiving partner is relaxed, by going slowly and in small increments, will help ease further possible discomfort.

For a girl, the first time may be anything from pleasurable to painful, regardless of whether it's with a guy or a girl. What the experience is like depends on a lot of factors, including the girl's body and the amount of foreplay involved.

If a girl does experience pain during sex, there could be a few reasons for it. First, if there is pain as the vagina is penetrated, the problem may be due to not having enough lubrication. This is a sensitive area and friction can hurt, which is why the body naturally gets wet and slippery through sexual arousal.

Spending a little more time with foreplay to help the vagina become lubricated naturally, or using an artificial lubricant such as KY Jelly, will help. Another possible reason for pain would be if the girl's hymen is still intact. If it is, it may be painful as the hymen stretches and breaks (there will also be some bleeding). To help ease any discomfort, a girl's partner should go slowly, as opposed to pushing fast all at once. A third possible reason for pain would be if something is wrong, for example, the girl has a yeast infection or an STD. Any pain experienced during sex because of an infection will last until the infection is treated.

You don't have to feel pain during sex; it is supposed to be enjoyable. If pain occurs at all, it should only be slight and temporary. It is important to talk with your partner and ensure that you are both physically and emotionally comfortable before continuing. And remember, you have only one first time. Make sure to think your decision through, and if you decide you're ready to have sex, protect yourself and your partner with a condom.

How do I tell my boyfriend (or girlfriend) that I'm not ready for sex?

Be honest and direct. Tell him or her how you feel and what you are thinking. A good boy- or girlfriend will want to know, and will want to respect your wishes. If you two are close enough to be considering sex, you are close enough to have an open and real conversation about your feelings. If you two can't, you may want to ask yourself if you're really ready to be intimate with each other.

Remember, you can always decide to be intimate later, but you can't ever take it back. So if you're not ready to have sex yet, tell your partner, and stick with the decision you have determined is right for you.

How old do I have to be to get birth control?

Birth control comes in many forms: abstinence, condoms, the pill, diaphragms, IUDs, and the ring, to name a few. You're never too young to practice abstinence, and you can get a condom at any age. As for prescription birth control methods such as the pill and others, the age you can get them depends on which state you live in. In many states, you don't have to be very old. (In fact, some doctors prescribe the pill to teen girls in order to reduce the pain and menstrual flow of their periods.) Your doctor can help determine what birth control is most appropriate for you given your age and circumstances. Don't be afraid to ask—in most states, a conversation about birth control is confidential, and your doctor will not tell anyone you asked about it. (To be sure, though, ask your doctor about his or her policy.)

How can I tell if a guy is a virgin?

The only way to find out if a guy is a virgin is to ask him. There is no other way—physically, appearance, or otherwise—to tell if a guy is a virgin.

Can STDs ever be completely gotten rid of?

It depends on the STD. Some STDs, such as chlamydia and gonorrhea, can be treated and fully cured. Others, such as HPV, genital herpes, and HIV, can be treated to reduce the symptoms, but cannot be cured.

If you think you may have an STD it is important to see a doctor immediately. Some STDs cause permanent damage that cannot be reversed, even if they can be cured. And keep in mind that some STDs do not show signs or symptoms in the infected person. If you suspect you've been exposed to an STD, even if you don't have noticeable symptoms, see a doctor.

STDs are also known as STIs, or sexually transmitted infections.

40

What does a circumcised penis look like? An uncircumcised one?

The difference between a circumcised and an uncircumcised penis has to do with foreskin. Foreskin is a loose fold of skin that covers the tip of the penis. Every baby boy is born with foreskin, and some parents have it removed by a doctor when the baby is only a few days old. This act of cutting off the foreskin and removing it is called circumcision.

So, a circumcised penis has no extra skin covering the tip of the penis. The tip (otherwise known as the glans or head) is fully visible in both the flaccid (limp) and erect states. An uncircumcised penis has its foreskin intact. When the penis is limp, the foreskin covers the tip of the penis. When the penis is erect, the foreskin naturally gets pulled back off the tip of the penis as it enlarges.

Both circumcised and uncircumcised penises are "normal" and "OK." One is not more "normal" than the other.

With all the condoms out there, how can I know which one to pick?

Condoms are the only protection that reduce the spread of STDs and help prevent pregnancy, so using them is a very responsible act. There are male and female condoms available, but let's talk about male condoms. For more about female condoms, see question 95.

There are many different options for condom users and many things to consider:

Material—Condoms are made from one of three materials: latex, polyurethane, or sheepskin. All three are equally effective in protecting against pregnancy, but they protect differently against STDs.

• Latex—What most people usually think of when they think "condom;" made of rubber; good protection against STDs; easy to find; most widely used; about $9 per dozen; can only be used with water-based lubricants; bad taste for use with oral sex.

- Polyurethane—Newest on the market; made from plastic; good protection against STDs; slightly less flexible than latex; may require more lubrication; thinner than latex and therefore increases sensitivity for some users; about $14 per dozen; can be used with oil- or water-based lubricants; no bad taste.
- Sheepskin—Oldest on the market; made of lamb intestine (not sheepskin); does not protect against STDs; contains natural, small pores that allow the transmission of viruses that cause STDs; the thinnest condom so generally feels the most natural; about $20 per dozen; can be used with oil- or water-based lubricants.

Size—Condoms come in a standard size, a smaller size which is a little snugger, and a mega or magnum size which is only about 2mm wider than the standard size.

Lubrication—Lubrication refers to a substance that makes the condom easier to put on and, for some people, more comfortable to use. Pre-lubricated condoms come with lubricant already inside the condom. If you buy condoms that are not pre-lubricated, you can add lubricant when you put the condom on. Water-based lubricants work well with all condoms; oil-based lubricants break down some condoms.

Condoms are also available with ribs or bumps to increase sensation and in different shapes: straight sides, form fitted (indented below the head of the penis), or flared (wider over the head of the penis), among others. Most are clear with no flavor, but you can also buy colored or flavored condoms.

Brand—Stick with a name brand.

Remember, if you get to the pharmacy and don't know which to buy, or can't make sense of all the options, the pharmacist can discreetly help you decide which condom is right for you.

How do I put a condom on?

Everyone is nervous the first time they put a condom on in front of, or for, their partner. If, however, you're comfortable having sex with your partner, hopefully you're comfortable enough to put a condom on in front of them. And if you mess up, it's no big deal; just throw the condom out, get another one, and try again.

A little practice before you start can help a lot. A guy can practice putting a condom on himself; girls can practice on a banana. (Really, it is good practice!)

Here's what you need to know:

- The penis must be erect.
- Open the condom packet, being sure not to tear the condom.
- If you want to add lubrication to the inside of the condom to increase sensitivity and reduce friction, put in a drop or two.

Most condoms have a reservoir tip to hold the ejaculation. Avoid getting air trapped in the reservoir when you put the condom on; air trapped in a condom could cause it to break. So, squeeze the tip on the condom between your thumb and forefinger and place it over the head of the erect penis. If the condom does not have a reservoir tip, make sure to leave about half an inch of space at the tip of the penis to collect the semen. Also make sure the roll is on the outside (that the condom is not inside out), or you won't be able to roll it down the penis.

Still squeezing the tip of the condom, use your other hand to unroll the condom down the length of the penis. Make sure to completely unroll it, covering as much of the penis as possible. Smooth out any air bubbles by rubbing your hand down the penis a few times.

If you want to, you can add more lubricant to the outside of the condom.

If the condom comes off or breaks during sex, withdraw the penis and condom immediately, wash the penis to remove any remaining sperm, and put on a new condom.

After ejaculation, while the penis is still partially erect, withdraw the penis from the vagina. Be sure to hold the condom in place at the base of the penis as you withdraw or you could pull out of the condom, accidentally leaving it in the vagina. Remove the condom only after you've fully withdrawn, and keep it and the penis away from your partner's body so no sperm are transferred. Wrap the condom in tissue and throw it in a trash can (it'll clog a toilet).

Remember—never, ever use a condom more than once, never store a condom in your wallet or car (the heat is very bad for them), and check the expiration date before using a condom.

What is the G-spot?

The G-spot (short for Gräfenberg spot) is a highly sensitive area in the vagina that is especially responsive to sexual stimulation. It is a 1- to 3-centimeter-long area along the upper vaginal wall (the side closest to the belly) that begins an inch or two from the opening. It is a bumpy area and feels like it has ridges. When a girl is aroused, the G-spot is said to swell slightly.

There is controversy about whether the G-spot actually exists. Doctors and scientists generally agree that such a uniquely sensitive area does not exist, but the general consensus of the public is that it does.

What can I do if I just had unprotected sex?

First, you're smart to recognize that you need to take action to protect yourself as much as you can, even after the fact. By having unprotected sex, you've exposed yourself to many risks, with sexually transmitted diseases and pregnancy being the biggest two. The right thing to do now is to take precautions that will protect you and your partner in the future.

Next, know that washing, rinsing, or douching will not help prevent pregnancy and will not wash away any STDs. Since you could now be pregnant, you may want to consider emergency contraception. Emergency contraception, otherwise known as the "morning-after pill," can help you avoid pregnancy if it is taken within 72 hours of having unprotected sex. It works best within 24 hours, however, and is about 90% effective. If you decide against taking this pill, make sure to take a pregnancy test in a few weeks to determine if you are pregnant.

Then you'll need to find out if you or your partner have transmitted an STD to each other. If you are having sex with someone, you have probably already discussed your health and theirs, but if you haven't, you really need to now. If either of you currently has an STD, you'll both need to get medical treatment immediately. Keep in mind that some infected people do not know that they have an STD and, therefore, they unknowingly transmit it to their partner. Also keep in mind that many STDs do not show their symptoms right away, and some are not detectable without the aid of a doctor. For these reasons, you'll need to examine yourself regularly for symptoms of STDs for the next few months and have a doctor examine you to determine if you are infected. Make sure to take this essential step in protecting yourself and your partner for the future. Also, make very sure to use protection going forward, especially during the time before you see the doctor, so you don't further risk spreading STDs.

Having unprotected sex is a risky thing to do. Putting a condom on may take an extra minute and may not seem like as much fun as having sex without one, but if you do have unprotected sex, you're exposing yourself to pregnancy, STDs, and months of worry, tests, and concern until a doctor can determine if you are healthy or not. It takes only one instance of unprotected sex to give you a sexually transmitted disease that will last a lifetime. In the future, protect yourself and your partner by using a condom.

Do all girls bleed the first time they have sex?

Some girls bleed the first time they have sex and some don't. Just like with every other aspect of sex, the answer depends on the person. Whether a girl bleeds or not has nothing to do with her virginity, or lack of virginity. You cannot tell if a girl is a virgin by whether or not she bleeds; some virgins will and some virgins won't.

Bleeding after having sex for the first time occurs when the hymen is stretched, or broken. If a girl's hymen had previously been broken (by rough exercise, tampon use, or something else) she will not experience bleeding after having sex for the first time. However, if her hymen was intact prior to having sex, she will have some bleeding. A girl can expect anywhere from a few drops to a light flow of blood when her hymen is broken.

I'm pregnant. What do I do now?

Girls who find out they're pregnant run the gamut of emotions from excited and thankful to terrified and surprised. Depending on your situation, you may experience some or all of these emotions. No matter the circumstances, every girl who finds out she's pregnant faces similar new responsibilities.

First, get support. This is one of the most life-changing experiences you will ever face. You will need the support of someone who loves you as you make decisions that will affect your future. If you were buying a car, picking a college to attend, or getting a job, you'd seek support and advice from knowledgeable people. Pregnancy is far more significant than any of those situations, so make sure you talk with someone you respect, love, and trust.

Next, get educated. Talk with your parents, partner, doctor, school nurse, or counselor. You will be making choices that you'll live with for the rest of your life, so be sure to know how they may affect you. Consider the emotional, physical, social, medical, financial, educational, and lifestyle changes that will result from your decisions.

Remember, no choice may feel totally right, but talking it through and earnestly weighing the options will help you determine what is best under the circumstances. The choices are complicated and deeply personal. And your decisions will have a life-changing impact on you and the baby, not just now, but for years to come. Think about the consequences of your choices and what is best in the long term. Get support, get educated, and make the best decision possible for both you and the baby. And no matter what choice you make, you will need medical care immediately.

Finally, if getting pregnant was not something you planned, use protection in the future to avoid being in the same situation.

What does a vagina look like? A penis?

A guy's genitals are pretty straightforward. The penis is made up of two parts: the shaft and the glans. The shaft is the main part of the penis, and the glans is the tip (or head) of the penis. Next, there are two testicles (sometimes called "balls") that are contained within a scrotum (the sack that holds the testicles). There is also the perineum, which is the area of skin between the scrotum and anus. Finally, there is the anus.

A girl's genitals require a little more explanation. The exterior genitalia, called a vulva, is comprised of many parts. The "outer lips," or labia majora, protect all the other parts of the vulva. Within these lips are another set of lips called the "inner lips," or labia minora. The inner lips are softer and engorge with blood when a girl is aroused. Within the inner lips, at the very top where they come together, is a clitoral hood. The clitoral hood covers and protects the clitoris. The clitoris is a sexual organ that has about twice as many nerve endings as the head of a penis and therefore is very sensitive to, and becomes stimulated by, sexual touch. The clitoris is approximately the size of a pencil eraser, but can be smaller or larger from girl to girl. Below the clitoris is the urinary opening and below the urinary opening is the vaginal opening. The area of skin between the vagina and the anus is called the perineum. Finally, there is the anus.

Genitals of both guys and girls can look dramatically different from one person to another. It is very normal for penises to vary in length, width, color, and shape, and for scrotums to vary as well. In girls, it is common for there to be wide variations in the appearance of the vulva. Differences in length, shape, fullness, texture, color, and elasticity are all very common.

My friend thinks she's gay. What should I say?

What would you want her to say to you if you told her something important, something that may be difficult to share at first? Like you, she probably is hoping for acceptance, understanding, and loyalty.

What you say may be influenced by how your friend feels. Is she happy to be "coming out" and excited to be sharing the information with you? Is she surprised and a little confused about who to tell and what to do next? Follow her lead in the conversation and listen closely to where her feelings are. Coming out at any age is hard and telling intimate details about yourself, especially when you don't know how it will be received, is scary. Like anyone, your friend is going to appreciate support and she obviously feels she can count on you to give it to her. She is the same great friend and person she was before she told you. Treat her as you would want a friend to treat you—with acceptance and respect.

An organization you and your friend may want to refer to is PFLAG (Parents, Families, and Friends of Lesbians and Gays). It provides good support and education in just these types of circumstances.

Can a girl get pregnant even if the penis doesn't enter her vagina?

Yes. Sperm are very good swimmers, and it is their job to swim around until they find an egg to penetrate. Even if the penis doesn't enter the vagina, if pre-ejaculate or ejaculate (semen, or "cum") gets anywhere near the vagina, the sperm can find their way in and up to an awaiting egg. Inserting fingers that previously touched semen into the vagina and ejaculating just outside of the vagina are examples of how a girl could get pregnant without a penis entering the vagina. Anytime there is sperm present, it is important that both partners take care to not transfer it into the vagina, or anywhere near it.

What is a hickey?

A hickey is a temporary bruise that is left on the skin. It is caused when forceful sucking or biting, while kissing, breaks blood vessels beneath the skin. Hickeys are red and purple in color, like any other bruise, and last for about 3 to 5 days, depending on their size and severity. There is no way to make hickeys disappear faster, but wearing makeup or covering them with a collared shirt can help conceal them from view.

How do steroids work?

Steroids are either naturally or artificially created hormones. They can have significant effects on the body's growth and development if they are combined with a rigorous exercise program and proper diet. There are many different types of steroids, but the most widely used is a synthetic testosterone (the male growth hormone).

People take steroids to get the extra hormones into their bodies, hoping to promote faster growth and development and bulk up the body's muscles by stimulating them to grow. Some people start taking them to either improve how they look or to improve their performance in sports. While steroids may enhance muscle mass, strength, and stamina, they don't improve a person's skill in sports.

Steroids come in different forms: injections, gels, oral drops, creams, and pills. Be clear, however, that steroids are drugs and are only legal with a prescription. Doctors may prescribe steroids to treat asthma, arthritis, allergies, and many other conditions.

Many steroids have serious side effects such as mood swings (anger and aggression), hallucinations, high blood pressure, and stunted final adult height. Using steroids can also lead to testicular shrinkage and an inability to get an erection (impotence) in guys, increased facial hair growth, and menstrual changes in girls. Certain side effects from steroid use can also result in death. These days, because of both the risks and the unfair advantage that steroid users have over other athletes, most professional sports organizations ban the use of steroids.

What does "sexual orientation" mean?

Sexual orientation refers to what gender a person is physically, emotionally, romantically, and sexually attracted to. Heterosexuals are attracted to the opposite gender, homosexuals are attracted to the same gender, and bisexuals are attracted to both genders.

Whether a person chooses his sexual orientation, or if it is predetermined at birth, is not completely agreed upon. According to the American Academy of Pediatrics, "Sexual orientation probably is not determined by any one factor but by a combination of genetic, hormonal and environmental influences."*

*"Sexual Orientation and Adolescents," American Academy of Pediatrics Clinical Report. Retrieved 2007.

One of my testicles hangs lower than the other. Is this normal?

Not to worry . . . this is very normal. The body is not symmetrical, and the testicles are no different. Most guys have one testicle that hangs lower than the other; it is also normal if one is slightly larger than the other. If, however, one testicle is significantly larger or harder than the other, you notice a lump, there is a change in appearance, or there is swelling or pain, see a doctor and have it checked out.

What is the discharge that sometimes comes
from my penis (or vagina)?

Let's talk about guys first. If there is discharge from the penis other than urine or semen, it is often the sign of a sexually transmitted disease. The discharge may be a little or a lot and be anywhere from clear to yellow to pale green. It may be accompanied by a rash, a need to urinate abnormally frequently, or a burning feeling when urinating. If a guy has any of these symptoms, he should see a doctor immediately for diagnosis and treatment.

Now, let's talk about girls. Some amount of discharge from the vagina is normal. Every day, a small amount of fluid flows out of the vagina, carrying out old cells and keeping the vagina clean. This normal discharge may be clear or milky white and doesn't smell bad. At times, the normal discharge may get a little thicker (like during ovulation or when a girl is sexually aroused).

If, however, the amount of discharge increases significantly, changes in color, or smells particularly bad, it could be the result of an infection. Other symptoms may include itching, burning, or irritation. If a girl has any of these symptoms, she should see a doctor for diagnosis and treatment.

If a person with an infection has unprotected sex, it is likely that the infection will get passed to the partner. So always get immediate treatment and keep yourself, and your partner if you have one, safe.

My mom tried drugs once, so why shouldn't I?

Trying drugs, like every other choice in life, is just that—a choice. You'll need to choose how carefully you're going to safeguard yourself from harm. You have only one life, and one body. There are some important considerations that may help you decide how well you'll treat them both.

First, remember that many of today's drugs are significantly stronger and faster acting than drugs of the past. Overdosing on fewer amounts of drugs is much easier to do today than it was in the past. Also, today's drugs can cause addiction much more quickly than previous drugs. With some of today's drugs, using them just once or a few times can cause a person to be addicted to them. Today's drugs are also more commonly combined with other dangerous street drugs that you don't even know are there. While you might think you are trying one drug, you may actually be taking in multiple drugs.

The effects of street drugs are also something to think about. Drugs can cause hallucinations, paranoia, an irregular heartbeat, loss of consciousness, seizures, brain damage, and death. Inhalants (such as glue, paint, and hair spray) can kill the user during the very first use. Other effects of inhalants include becoming addicted quickly, loss of hearing, loss of sense of smell, and severe toxic reactions. All street drugs affect the brain and all drugs damage the body.

Most likely, when the opportunity arises for you to walk away from trying drugs, good advice from a trusted adult will not be around. More likely, you'll be with other teens who are facing the same choice. Consider your options and their consequences carefully beforehand so that when the time comes, you'll already know what you want to do. Make the choice to keep yourself safe, and alive. Nobody who ever became addicted to drugs, or died using them, thought they would before they tried them the first time.

Do I have to swallow?

Any time a question about sex starts with "Do I have to . . . ," the answer is no. You never have to do anything you don't want to do.

When a guy or girl talks about "swallowing," it refers to swallowing a guy's ejaculation after performing oral sex on him. The options are to swallow it, spit it out, or avoid getting it in your mouth in the first place. What you do is up to you.

A girl cannot get pregnant from performing oral sex, whether or not she swallows. STDs, however, can be transferred to and from either partner during oral sex. To decrease the risk of transferring STDs or infections, use a condom or a female condom with your partner.

What is the morning-after pill?

Emergency contraception, otherwise known as the "morning-after pill," can prevent a girl from getting pregnant if it is taken within 72 hours of having sex. It works best within 24 hours, however. This pill is about 90% effective and the most common side effects are nausea and vomiting.

Emergency contraception is meant to be used only very occasionally, as the name implies. These pills contain the same hormones that birth control pills contain, but in higher levels. The higher doses of hormones prevent pregnancy by (1) preventing the ovaries from releasing an egg, (2) preventing the fertilization of the egg, or (3) preventing implantation by altering the lining of the womb so a fertilized egg can't embed itself there.

There are multiple brands of morning-after pills that are approved by the Federal Drug Administration (FDA) and are safe to take. Girls (or guys) of any age can buy it over the counter without a prescription.

How do you kiss?

For someone who has never kissed or been kissed, it can look a little intimi-
dating. How do you know when to lean in, which side do you tilt your head
to, how hard or soft should it be, tongue or no tongue—it's a lot to think
about. The good news is that it's much simpler than it looks.

All people kiss differently, but there are a few things you can do to help
the first time go smoothly. First, relax and take a deep breath; when the time
is right for you and your partner, you'll sense it. Read your partner's body
language and follow his or her lead. Your partner may indicate readiness by
leaning in closer, looking at you in a certain way, or putting an arm around
you. When you are about to kiss, tilt your head to one side to avoid bumping
noses, and gently press your lips together.

That's all there is to it. After a few times, it will feel natural and you'll
wonder why you ever worried in the first place!

What is anal sex?

Anal sex is when a guy inserts his penis into his partner's anus. The term is sometimes used to describe other sexual encounters that include the anus, such as when a girl penetrates her partner with a dildo.

The anus has thousands of nerve endings in and around it that make it very sensitive. Some people enjoy being stimulated in this erogenous zone and others don't; both viewpoints are common.

Guys and girls who engage in anal sex will find it more comfortable if they use lubrication. Otherwise, it could hurt because the anus doesn't produce enough lubrication on its own to make sex comfortable. Be sure to use a water-based lubricant that won't break down the condom.

I'm unsure about my sexual orientation. What do I do?

If you're not sure about your sexual orientation, give yourself some more time to figure it out. With time, you will begin to notice yourself becoming attracted to people, and your orientation will show itself to you. There is no right or wrong orientation; there is only what is right for you. Some guys and girls are sure about their orientation early on; for others it takes time, doubt, and exploration. Discover your feelings and you'll discover your orientation. No matter what your orientation is, remember that it is the right orientation for you and it's great that you discovered it. Being comfortable and happy with yourself (self-acceptance) is very important.

What's the best way to prevent catching an STD?

The best way to prevent getting a sexually transmitted disease is to practice abstinence (not having vaginal, oral, or anal sex). For guys and gals who are sexually active, there are ways to minimize the risk of catching an STD:

- Choose a partner who has limited his or her number of previous partners, and keep your number of partners limited as well.
- Ask your partner if he or she is currently uninfected and only having sex with you. Keep in mind that your partner could have an STD and not yet know it, since symptoms of an STD don't always appear right away.
- Talk with your partner about safe sex, his or her sexual history, and care he or she has taken in the past to prevent infection. If you can't talk openly about these things to prevent the possible spread of an STD, rethink if you are ready to have sex with this person.
- Use a condom. This is very important and will significantly reduce the risk of transferring an STD. However, be aware that a condom

may not cover the entire infected area of a person, so, while a condom is great protection, it is not a guarantee. That is why talking to your partner and choosing a safe partner are such important considerations.

- Do not use a spermicide; they are no longer recommended. Spermicides can actually irritate the tissue in the vagina and make it easier to transfer an STD.
- Get regular (at least yearly) exams to ensure you are not infected. If you are infected, you must tell your partner immediately so he or she can get medical treatment as soon as possible.

It should be noted that some STDs are transferred through actions as simple as kissing (herpes, for instance) or heavy touching (genital warts can be transferred this way). Although it is unrealistic to think that guys and girls will abstain from kissing and touching for the rest of their lives, if you choose a partner carefully and know his or her history, you will continue to reduce your risk of catching an STD. If you think you've been exposed to an STD, see your doctor immediately.

What makes a penis get erect?

An erection is sometimes called "a boner," even though there is no bone in the penis. The penis is made of soft, spongy tissue that contains lots of small blood vessels and nerve endings.

When a guy is sexually aroused, blood vessels in the penis fill with blood, causing the penis to swell and grow in size. The previously soft penis becomes hard and rises up. This is what is known as an erection. Once a guy ejaculates, or if he becomes un-aroused, the penis will go back to its normal flaccid, or limp, state.

What's a clitoris and is it important?

The clitoris is a female sexual organ. Its sole purpose is to bring about sexual pleasure and orgasm in girls. It is considered, in some ways, the female equivalent of a guy's penis. The clitoris has approximately 8,000 nerve fibers (about twice as many as the penis); therefore, stimulating it can feel exceptionally good to some girls. Other girls find it almost too sensitive and prefer that the clitoris not be directly stimulated.

The clitoris is protected by a fold of skin called the clitoral hood. This hood is located just below the folds of the labia minora, at the very top where they come together. While the size of the clitoris varies from girl to girl, it is generally about the size of a pencil eraser and protrudes slightly when aroused. When orgasm takes place, muscles around the clitoris and vagina contract rhythmically.

Do girls ejaculate?

This is a topic of debate; some people say yes and some say no. When a guy experiences the feeling of an orgasm, he ejaculates (that is, ejects semen). When a girl has an orgasm, she does not usually eject fluid. Her body will produce lubrication as she is stimulated and aroused during sexual activity, but this is different from ejaculating.

Some research suggests that girls can and do ejaculate, but only a small percentage of girls say that they have. Very little medical research has addressed where the ejaculate (if there is any) originates from, but girls who report ejaculating say that it comes out of the urethra. Regardless of whether or not girls ejaculate, they definitely experience orgasms and the pleasurable feelings associated with them.

How often do people have sex?

This answer will vary greatly from person to person. On average, guys and girls who are in a committed relationship report having sex about two or three times per week. That said, some people haven't had sex in years, and others have sex multiple times per day. There is no "normal" in this area; it is whatever you and your partner decide.

If I talk to my doctor about having sex, will he or she tell my parents?

Every state has different guidelines that doctors must follow when it comes to keeping conversations they have with teen patients confidential. For example, one state may require the patient to be older than 12 for conversations to be confidential, whereas another state may require the patient to be 15. The best way to definitively know if your doctor will keep your conversations confidential is to call the doctor's office and ask. Also be sure to ask under what circumstances the doctor might have to share, by law, information you tell him or her. The doctor or office staff will be happy to tell you about their policies.

Does the withdrawal method of birth control work?

Also called "pulling out," the withdrawal method is when a guy removes his penis from the vagina just before he is about to ejaculate. It is a very unreliable form of birth control, for a few reasons. First, pre-ejaculate, which is discharged prior to ejaculation, contains sperm and can get a girl pregnant. Second, hoping the guy pulls out in time is risky. And even if the guy ejaculates outside the vagina, there is still a risk of pregnancy. Finally, this method doesn't protect against STDs. So while pulling out can work, it is very unsafe.

How do I tell my mom or dad that I'm ready to have sex?

Good for you for wanting to talk about such an important decision. That you are ready to discuss your choice with a trusted adult shows that you're thinking maturely.

Be straightforward about your thoughts, feelings, and actions. Hit on the big points—that you want to be honest and keep her (or him) in the loop about your life, that you are smart enough to use protection every time you have sex, and that you have thought about the different possible consequences of your actions, like pregnancy and STDs. (If you haven't thought of these things, you're not ready to have sex yet.) Be prepared for her to ask you questions about what you've said, and also be prepared to give her some time to think about your answers. After all, while you've probably been thinking about this conversation for a while, it may come as a surprise to her.

What is a French kiss?

A French kiss is when partners touch their tongues to each other's lips, tongue, and inside of the mouth. It is a very passionate kiss and often lasts longer than brief kisses on the lips.

Generally, STDs are not spread by kissing, but because more saliva is exchanged during a French kiss, the chances of catching an STD are higher than they are with a less intimate kiss. Herpes and mononucleosis (mono) are two examples of orally transmitted diseases that can be spread through French kissing.

70

How can I ask my partner to get tested for STDs?

Talking about getting tested for STDs can be uncomfortable at first, but if you can't talk to your partner about it, you aren't ready to have sex. So, be up front with your partner. Tell him or her that you want to keep both of you safe. Tell your partner that you want to talk about infections that, if transferred, could stay with you for your entire life. Also say that risking your health is unnecessary and that getting tested is a sign of maturity, respect, and preparedness to engage in sex. Finally, remind your partner that many new infections don't show symptoms right away and that old infections sometimes don't reappear for a long time, even though they are still there. If your partner doesn't want to get tested, don't have sex with him or her; you'd only be putting yourself at risk.

Does masturbating have any long-term, negative effects?

Masturbation is a safe, common, and healthy sexual act. It is nothing to feel guilty about. Most people, both guys and girls, masturbate. Some may try it once; others may masturbate every day. Masturbation is perfectly healthy. Just like with any behavior, however, if it begins to interfere with your normal, daily activities, it is not good for you.

There are many myths about masturbating, such as that it can lead to blindness, hairy palms, or even death. These myths are completely false. In fact, some research suggests that masturbation has health benefits such as temporary relief of stress, depression, and insomnia (the inability to sleep).

Does the size of a guy's foot really predict his penis size?

No, not at all. This is a common myth, but it is not true. You also cannot predict penis size from the size of a guy's nose or hand, or his height, weight, or build.

Are my labia normal?

Labia are the lip-shaped folds of tissue on either side of the vulva (the female external genitalia). There is an outer pair of labia (labia majora) and within them, on either side of the vaginal opening, is an inner pair of labia (labia minora). Many girls wonder if their labia are normal, or not, because labia can look very different from one girl to the next.

The outer labia are covered with pubic hair and are soft, fatty, and can be somewhat plump, while the inner lips are generally thinner. Beyond that, there is a wide range of differences in how labia appear and all are normal. Labia differ in:

- Size—plump or thin, long or short
- Texture—smooth or bumpy, loose or elastic
- Color—darker, pinker, or the same color as the surrounding skin
- Shape—flat or ruffled, closed or laying farther apart

Also, some inner labia protrude through the outer labia and others don't.

Sometimes, too, the labia are asymmetrical and a person has a large lip on one side and almost none on the other. All of these variations in the appearance of the labia are common and normal.

Does drinking a beer get you less drunk than drinking a shot of liquor?

The answer to this question is a little complicated.

A standard serving of beer is 12 ounces (can, bottle, or poured), of wine is 5 ounces, and of liquor is 1½ ounces (in a mixed drink or a straight shot). If the liquor is 80 proof (that is, 40% alcohol), then each of the servings of beer, wine, and liquor contains the same amount of alcohol. It makes sense that someone might think "a drink is a drink is a drink" and assume that each would get a person drunk at the same rate. In theory this is right, but in reality and everyday practice, it is wrong.

Even though the drinks contain the same amount of alcohol, the truth is that they are not all the same. A person will get full on beer before wine or liquor, because he or she has to drink more liquid to get the same amount of alcohol. Another difference is that a person can drink a straight shot of alcohol faster than a beer or a glass of wine. People drinking shots may, therefore, feel the effects sooner. Also, a beer comes in a premeasured can or bottle. With liquor, if a bartender doesn't measure how much is being poured, more than 1½ ounces may get poured into a drink. Finally, not all alcohol is 80 proof; a lot of alcohol is actually stronger and is, therefore, more potent.

Remember that the legal drinking age in every state is 21. And never, ever drive if you've had a drink. If you do, you are risking both your life and the lives of others.

What is an aphrodisiac?

An aphrodisiac is anything that arouses or increases a person's sexual desire. It could be a food, drink, scent, attitude, or even the moon's cycle. While there isn't any medical evidence to support the claim that over-the-counter items (as opposed to prescription medications) can increase sexual desire, a lot of people feel they do. Oysters, licorice, power, perfume, chocolate, a full moon, and figs are examples of what some people consider natural aphrodisiacs.

People bully me. What can I do?

It's wrong, but many guys and girls are bullied these days. The pain and em-barrassment that come with bullying can do a lot of damage to a person's self-esteem and happiness. There are two ways to decrease the harmful ef-fects of bullying: (1) decrease the bullying itself, and (2) decrease the ef-fect it has on you.

It would be great if you could simply go to the bully and say, "Hey, that hurts my feelings, please stop." It is an honest, direct, and mature approach and, hopefully, would stop the bullying. However, in case that approach doesn't work, let's discuss some other options. First, try disarming bullies by taking away their ammunition; when they bully you, ignore them. It won't be easy, but if you don't react to their meanness, they may get bored and soon stop the bullying. You could also try responding with humor and make a joke of the situation.

If these alternatives don't decrease the bullying, ask an adult for help. Pick an adult who will listen to your concerns and feelings—one who will ad-dress them. Tell your parents, family, or school counselor. Be specific about what the bully has said or done. If you don't get the help you need, go to another adult and ask again. Bullying is a significant issue, and sometimes the first person you tell may not understand how much pain it really causes you. Keep asking until you find an adult who is successful in helping you stop the bullying.

In addition to decreasing the bullying itself, you can also work on decreasing the effect it has on you. First, realize that anybody who is being mean is most likely in a lot of pain themselves—maybe they are bullied at home or at school, or maybe they're insecure. People who are happy do not try to make others unhappy; only people who are hurting try to hurt others. Realize that the bully is a sad person who is hurting.

Next, be confident about who you are. Tell yourself how great you are and know that you are great, no matter what a bully may say about you. There will always be sad people who try to make others sad; you can't lead your life allowing their words to determine your happiness level and how you feel about yourself. If you do, your happiness will always depend on somebody else's mean mood! And if you listen to the bullies who only have negative words for people, you will miss out on knowing all the positive and wonderful things about yourself. Know who you are and don't let a bully take that from you. Finally, stay in control of your behaviors and feelings and focus on more positive things. Remember—try to lessen both the bullying and the effect it has on you!

What is the difference between HIV and AIDS?

"HIV" stands for human immunodeficiency virus. It is the virus that causes AIDS. HIV is transferred when blood, vaginal fluids, semen, or breast milk of an infected person contacts an uninfected person's mucous membranes or an area of broken skin. Areas that are made of mucous membranes include the vagina, the opening of the penis, anus, mouth, nose, and eyes. HIV can also be transferred from a mom to her baby during pregnancy, childbirth, or breastfeeding. Some other examples of ways HIV can be transferred include sharing drug needles; having unprotected vaginal, anal, or oral sex with an infected partner; and getting infected blood in a cut.

"AIDS" stands for acquired immune deficiency syndrome. It develops from the HIV infection and weakens a person's immune system (the body's system that fights off infections, foreign substances, and diseases). People with AIDS will have a lot of difficulty recovering from common ailments, such as the flu, that would not normally be a problem for people with healthy immune systems. They may also develop certain new infections or cancers. Although there are medications available to slow down the progression of the disease, there is still no cure for AIDS, and people die of it every day.

Don't hesitate to be friends with someone who has HIV or AIDS. You are safe as long as no blood or body fluids are transferred.

78

I've thought seriously about suicide. What should I do?

You're already taking the first and most important step—you're realizing that you need help and support. Now, seek out a trusted adult (parent, doctor, or counselor) and tell him or her how you feel. Ask the person to help you get the counseling and resources you'll need to overcome the sadness and despair that accompanies thoughts of suicide.

Suicide is not an answer; it is an end before an answer can be found. Wanting to die means you want a change, but make it a positive change, not a negative one. With help, you will be able to overcome the pain you are currently in and live a happier life.

If you want help but are not yet ready to talk with someone face to face, a good resource is the National Suicide Prevention Lifeline. The number is 1-800-273-TALK (1-800-273-8255).

How much can I drink before I shouldn't drive?

You should never mix drinking and driving—ever. If you've never done it, you may not know how lucky you are right now. And if you have done it and survived, consider yourself lucky. Many others have done it only once, and died, or injured or killed someone else. After all, it's not just yourself you should consider if you drink and get in a car: you risk the lives of every driver and pedestrian you pass. Imagine killing someone and living with that guilt for the rest of your life. All of a sudden a taxi fare, or a call to your parents, may not seem so bad.

In most states, if you've had even one drink, you are probably over the legal alcohol limit, making it illegal to drive. Your exact tolerance would depend on factors such as weight, how many drinks you had, and how long it had been since your last drink. It is safe to assume, however, that one drink will put you in jeopardy.

The ironic part is that alcohol often makes many people feel invincible, even as it is impairing their senses. So make an agreement with yourself, when you're sober, to never drink and drive. Will it be hard to call your parents, tell them you've been drinking, and ask for a ride? Of course, it will. Will you be in trouble? Maybe, but even if your parents are upset that you drank, they will probably be proud of you for making the good decision not to drive.

If you've used drugs, the same advice applies.

Remember, never be a passenger in a car with a driver who has been drinking or using drugs.

Which helps cure a hangover faster—aspirin or coffee?

Neither, really. Hangovers are the disagreeable physical effects of drinking too much alcohol in too short a time. Symptoms of a hangover include headaches, sensitivity to light and sound, weakness, dehydration, red eyes, nausea and vomiting, irritability, dizziness, thirst, body aches, and diarrhea. They only get better with rest, time, and liquids. Rest is needed so your body can recuperate from the beating it went through. Time is needed for your body to metabolize the alcohol and get rid of it. Liquids such as water, sports drinks, and juices are needed to rehydrate your dehydrated body.

Aspirin will help calm your headache, but that is all it will do; the hangover and all its other symptoms will still be there. Aspirin may also irritate your already upset stomach. As for coffee, it will only make you more awake; it will not make you more clear headed or coordinated. Since rest is one of the things a person with a hangover needs most, coffee to help get rid of a hangover is not a good idea. Remember—rest, time, and liquids.

What does "popping the cherry" mean?

"Popping the cherry" is a slang term meaning to have sex with a virgin girl. It refers to breaking ("popping") the hymen ("cherry") of a virgin.

My vagina has a certain odor. Is this normal?

During and after puberty, there is a small amount of discharge released from the vagina each day. It may be clear or white, or sometimes a bit of both. This discharge is normal and is how the vagina cleans itself.

There is also a certain amount of odor that is normally present. The smell isn't usually unpleasant or pleasant; it's just there. If the odor becomes unpleasant, "fishy" smelling, or noticeably strong even with daily showers, you should see a doctor. The unpleasant odor could be a sign of an infection of the vagina or vulva. If there is an infection, your daily discharge will usually, but not always, be thicker than normal and may be yellowish or greenish. An unusual discharge may also be a sign of a sexually transmitted disease, whether there is an unpleasant odor or not. If you are concerned about a change in your normal discharge, see a doctor.

Be assured that concerns like this are commonplace and nothing to be embarrassed about. Doctors see patients for these symptoms all the time and it's important that you make an appointment as soon as you have a concern. In most cases of infection, treatment is relatively fast and simple if it takes place right away.

How can I prevent premature ejaculation?

"Premature ejaculation" is when a guy regularly ejaculates sooner than he or his partner wants him to. It affects approximately one out of every three guys.

The first thing to do to prevent premature ejaculation is to openly communicate with your partner. Talk about your expectations, desires, and how long it takes both of you to become sexually excited enough to orgasm. Also talk about what, if any, different techniques you and your partner could use to bring you both to orgasm at the same time. You could also try masturbating and ejaculating a few hours before engaging in sex so that you're not as sexually charged during sex, thereby helping delay your orgasm. If none of this helps prevent the premature ejaculation, talk with your doctor about treatments. Possible treatments may include medications, sexual counseling, and techniques you can learn that help to delay ejaculation.

Can a guy who hasn't gone through puberty ejaculate?

A guy or girl who hasn't started puberty is called "pre-pubescent." A pre-pubescent guy can orgasm, but he can't ejaculate. It is only after a boy has started puberty and is producing semen that he can ejaculate. Until this time, his orgasms are referred to as "dry" because there is no discharge.

#

What is cunnilingus?

"Cunnilingus" is the formal term for performing oral sex on a girl.

What do I say to my friend to help her stop cutting herself?

Reports show that 15–17% of U.S. teens and young adults report having a history of self-injury, and it is growing more prevalent amongst teens.

"Cutting" is when a guy or girl uses a sharp object to injure themselves by slicing or cutting their own skin until they bleed. Guys and girls don't cut themselves for attention. In fact, they often try to hide their cuts, injuring themselves in places that can be concealed from friends and family.

Cutters cut themselves because they are experiencing a pain so great that they don't know how to cope with it in a healthy way. Fifty-five percent of people who injure themselves say they do so to "get my mind off my problems." They may also cut to relieve stress, anxiety, anger, or depression. Cutting is a significant problem that requires equally significant support, therapy, and intervention. (One study found that 70% of teens who self-injured had also attempted suicide at least once.)

Reassure your friend that you are still a friend, and that your friendship is not in jeopardy. Help your friend understand that he or she needs to seek help from parents or other adults. If your friend is too consumed with negative feelings to seek help, you will need to step up and get an adult's help yourself. It may be hard, but it is in your friend's best interest to get professional support and therapeutic assistance immediately. Cutting doesn't usually get better without help. With help, it is treatable and recovery is possible.

If you have a friend who hasn't confided in you but whom you suspect of cutting, talk with them about it. Often, it is too hard for someone to ask for help in a situation like this, but they are glad to receive it once it's offered.

My breasts are lumpy. Is this normal?

Breasts are somewhat lumpy by nature because they are made up of fibrous and fatty tissue, milk glands, and milk ducts. These contribute to breasts being uneven in texture below the skin, which is perfectly normal. If, however, there is a distinct or protruding lump of any size, or any change to how your breasts normally look and feel, then you may want to contact your doctor. While the majority of the lumps girls find are noncancerous, any concerns can best be addressed by a doctor.

She can't get pregnant, so do I need to wear a condom when having anal sex?

Yes, you definitely need to wear a condom.

You are only partially correct when you say that a girl can't get pregnant by having anal sex. While she can't get pregnant directly from having anal sex, semen can seep out of the anus and toward the vaginal opening. The sperm can then "swim" into and up the vagina and impregnate the girl. So, pregnancy is a possible consequence of having unprotected anal sex; therefore, you need to wear a condom.

Another important reason to wear a condom when having anal sex is to prevent the spread of STDs. The anus is a high-risk area for many STDs including HIV, gonorrhea, herpes, syphilis, hepatitis B, and chlamydia. It is also an area full of bacteria, so if you are going to have anal sex, be sure to use a condom every time.

Is it OK to go out with my friend's ex if my friend was the one who dumped the person?

It depends on how your friend would feel about your dating her ex, and how you would feel about yourself if you did it. Even if your friend did the dumping, that doesn't mean she didn't really care about the person. She may still care for her ex, could have gone through a lot of pain in the breakup, or maybe would just feel betrayed if you went out with him. Ask yourself if you would like it if your friend went out with your ex. Would it hurt to see them together? Would you still want to hang out with her? Treat your friend like you'd want to be treated—which may mean you need to find somebody else to date!

Why do my parents always tell me to wait before having sex?

The decision to have sex is a huge and irreversible one. Once you give your virginity to a partner, you can never regain it. Anytime a guy or girl is considering such an enormous decision, it is natural for a parent to suggest waiting. Think of it this way . . . if you wait, you can always do it later, but if you have sex now, there is no going back.

Your parents want you to be sure that you are making the best decision in the long run, not the best decision for you today. And let's face it . . . if you're thinking about having sex, there are some pretty strong sexual urges that are influencing you. Your parents are trying to help you think not only about the immediate urges, but also about the long-term consequences. They want you to take the time to consider things like:

- The consequences of pregnancy and the decisions you'd have to face as a result. Would you keep the baby? Could you finish school? Could you get a job to pay the bills? How would you get medical treatment?

- Would you be happy later, no matter what choice you made, knowing you had to make it at such a young age?
- Coping with the emotional, physical, social, psychological, and spiritual issues that would result from an unplanned pregnancy.
- The consequences of getting an STD and the decisions you'd have to face possibly having a lifelong and incurable disease.
- Having to tell each and every future, potential partner about your transmittable disease.
- The possibly painful physical symptoms of your STD reoccurring at random times throughout your life.
- Getting and paying for your medical treatment.

These consequences and decisions are often overshadowed by the sexual urges guys and girls experience when they begin thinking about having sex. Your parents want you to take some extra time to think about your decision before you make it so that you can be sure it is the best long-term decision for you.

How do I come out to my parents?

First, know that every person reacts differently to big news, and it may take your parents some time to get used to your coming out. Next, be aware that there are common emotional phases that families may go through, in part or in whole, when a child "comes out." These phases are shock, denial, guilt, expression of their feelings, making a decision, and true acceptance. Some families never experience the first three stages, while others never experience the last. Every family's ability to be supportive is unique, but anticipating the phases your family may go through will benefit everybody. Finally, be patient. It has probably taken you a while to be sure of your sexual orientation, and it may take your parents a while, too.

If you think they may cut ties with you, that coming out would do irreparable damage to your relationship, or that other extreme consequences may occur, you may want to wait until you feel the situation is better before coming out.

If, however, you have determined that it is the right time to come out, tell your parents directly, confidently, and honestly. Tell them the truth—that you are proud of who you are and that you would like their support, love, and understanding. Pick a time when you can talk without interruption or distractions, and be prepared to answer a lot of questions.

Two websites that have a lot of this information, and more resources and links to supportive organizations in your area, are www.outproud.org and www.pflag.org.

Where can I get free birth control?

Free condoms are available from a number of sources, but you may have to search a little to find them. Some schools offer free condoms through the school nurse. If your school doesn't, the nurse will be able to direct you to where you can get them in your area. Also, many clinics offer free condoms. You can call your state's Department of Health to get contact numbers for clinics near you. Other birth control, such as the pill, diaphragm, or IUD, is available by prescription only and is not given out for free.

How many times can a girl orgasm during sex? A guy?

Having a second orgasm (or third, or fourth) soon after the first one, without the body relaxing in between, is referred to as having multiple orgasms. It is common for girls to experience multiple orgasms because their bodies can "recover" between orgasms fairly quickly. That said, it's also just as normal for a girl to never have multiple orgasms. It just depends on the girl.

Guys can also have more than one orgasm during sex, but they usually have just one because they require a longer time to recover between orgasms.

I've heard that pot isn't as dangerous as some other drugs . . . true or false?

Marijuana, or "pot," has often been suggested to be one of the "safer" drugs when compared to drugs that have more significant side effects. However, having fewer dangerous effects than cocaine and heroin does not mean marijuana is safe; it just means it is safer than other extremely harmful drugs.

Smoking pot can alter a person's brain, resulting in changes to mood, perception, and behavior. It can also alter a person's physical and biochemical functioning. Specifically, pot has been shown to impair memory and the ability to learn, increase heart rate, and decrease problem-solving skills. It can also distort thinking, decrease motor coordination, increase anxiety, lower a person's sex drive, delay reaction times, and decrease sperm count in guys. It can even lead to panic attacks and paranoia, especially with new users.

Marijuana is also addictive, with an estimated 9% of all users becoming addicted. The addiction rate increases to as much as 25–50% for daily users.

The younger a person starts, the greater the likelihood of addiction; one in six people who start in their teens becomes addicted. While pot may not technically be as risky as some other drugs, it is still a very dangerous and harmful drug.

How do I use a female condom?

A female condom is a sheath of polyurethane that girls wear during sex to protect against pregnancy and the transfer of STDs. They are about 6.5 inches long, have a ring on either end, and are pre-lubricated to make them easier to insert into the vagina. It is safe to add more lubricant to the condom, if needed.

Female condoms are 95% effective if used correctly and are best used for vaginal sex only. They are difficult to use for anal sex. An advantage of the female condom over a male condom is that it can be inserted in advance of a sexual encounter.

To use a female condom:

- Check the expiration date.
- Remove the condom from its package, making sure the inner ring is inside the sheath and that the sheath is extended. Add more lubricant, as desired.
- Pinch the inner ring into an oval shape.

- With the ring pinched, insert it into the vagina far enough that it won't pop out.
- Insert one finger into the exposed end of the condom and gently push it into the vagina as far as it will go. The inner ring, which has now popped back to a circular shape, will hold the condom securely in the vagina during sex. The outer ring will remain outside the vagina and secure it there.
- Hold the outer ring in place as the penis is initially inserted into the vagina so that the penis goes into the condom, not around it.
- When you're ready to remove the condom, pull on the outer ring, making sure not to expose your genitalia to any semen.

Does a guy have to go to a special doctor like a girl does?

In addition to their general doctor, most girls begin seeing a gynecologist at some point in their lives. A gynecologist is a doctor who specializes in health care for women. Girls go to a gynecologist for annual checkups, to discuss any concerns they may have, and to get prescription birth control. Guys do not have an equivalent specialist. Unless he has a medical concern, a guy's annual visit with his general practitioner is usually enough.

97

I said "no" to sex and my partner didn't stop. What do I do now?

Tell a trusted adult, immediately. Tell your parents, your doctor, your school nurse or counselor, a teacher, or another trusted adult, but tell them immediately. You will need the advice and guidance of an adult who can help you get the emotional support and medical treatment you need. Some of the help you may want is time sensitive, like the morning-after pill (taken to avoid becoming pregnant). Other support and treatment may not be as critically time sensitive, but it is still very important. You will need support as you cope with your emotions, possible medical issues, and possible legal issues. Tell someone you trust, someone who can help you get the resources you will need to address and cope with what happened, and to heal.

Can a girl get pregnant if a guy ejaculates next to her in a pool?

No. A girl cannot get pregnant if a guy ejaculates next to her in a pool, even if it is very near her. Being close to semen is not enough to get a girl pregnant. The semen would have to come in direct contact with her vulva for there to be a chance of pregnancy.

If, however, a girl has sex in a pool, she could get pregnant. Having sex in a pool, shower, or Jacuzzi does not prevent a girl from getting pregnant; that is a myth.

Can I really die from huffing?

Absolutely. Many guys and girls die from huffing every year, and countless others do permanent harm to themselves.

Huffing is when someone inhales common household chemicals in order to get high. It is on the rise because people underestimate the risks, it's easy to access, and parents often don't know what huffing is so they don't readily discuss its dangers.

Inhalants can be found throughout any house. Commonly abused inhalants include gasoline, rubber cement, nail polish remover, glue, and lighter fluid. Other common inhalants are markers, aerosol from vegetable cooking sprays, spray paint, whipped cream, and compressed air (like the kind used to blow dust off computers). Even helium is an inhalant that has caused death. Warning signs that someone is huffing may include regular purchases of a common inhalant for no apparent use; paint stains on clothing, fingers, or the mouth; a chemical smell on the breath; watery eyes; and a dazed or dizzy appearance.

The dangers of huffing are dramatic and often deadly. When huffed, inhalants depress the central nervous system, thereby giving the user a "rush" that is quickly followed by wooziness. Users sometimes pass out completely and suffocate on the bag they were huffing from. They can also die of cardiac arrest because inhalants can cause an irregular heartbeat. If users don't die, they may face permanent brain damage (including cell death, memory impairment, and learning disabilities) or damage to their heart, liver, kidneys, and other organs. They may also permanently impair their vision, speech, coordination, and hearing. The risks of permanent, physical damage or sudden death are prevalent with each and every use. Whether it's the first huff or the hundredth, every time a user huffs, he or she risks their life.

How long does sex usually last?

There is no set answer to this because there is no "usually" when referring to how long sex lasts. Some guys and girls begin with foreplay and continue for hours. Others may want to orgasm as fast as possible and be done in a matter of minutes. How long sex lasts is a decision that partners make each time they have sex.

Glossary

abstinence: not having vaginal, oral, or anal sex

AIDS: acquired immune deficiency syndrome; a disease of the immune system that increases a person's vulnerability to infections

anal sex: when a man inserts his penis, or a woman inserts a dildo, into a partner's anus

anorexia: an eating disorder characterized by a fear of becoming fat, a distorted body image, an unwillingness to eat, and excessive dieting; anorexia nervosa

aphrodisiac: anything that arouses or increases a person's sexual desire

bulimia: an eating disorder characterized by binge eating followed by self-induced vomiting that is meant to prevent weight gain

circumcision: the act of cutting the foreskin off a newborn's penis

clitoral hood: fold of skin that covers and protects the clitoris

clitoris: female sexual organ that is very sensitive and becomes stimulated by sexual touch; in relation to sensitivity and arousal, it is the female equivalent of a penis

cold sore: a blister on the lips or mouth that is caused by herpes simplex; fever blister

coming out: to publicly acknowledge being homosexual

cum: semen; ejaculate

cunnilingus: the act of performing oral sex on a girl

depression: a state of despair that lasts for more than two weeks and is so severe that it disrupts a person's life; extreme unhappiness

dildo: an artificial penis

douching: when a girl squeezes a mixture of water and either a mild soap or vinegar into her vagina to cleanse it

ejaculation: when semen is ejected from the penis

erection: an erect penis; a penis that has grown, become hard, and risen up in response to sexual arousal

fellatio: the act of performing oral sex on a guy

French kiss: when partners touch their tongues to each other's lips, tongue, and inside of the mouth

G-spot: a highly sensitive area in the vagina that is especially responsive to sexual stimulation

gynecologist: a doctor who specializes in health care for women

hangover: the disagreeable physical effects of drinking too much alcohol in too short a time

hickey: a temporary bruise that is left on the skin from forceful sucking or biting while kissing

HIV: human immunodeficiency virus; the virus that causes AIDS

huffing: when a person inhales common, household chemicals in order to get high

hymen: a very thin and flexible membrane or tissue that stretches across the opening of the vagina, partially covering it

immune system: the body's system that fights off infections, foreign substances, and diseases

impotence: an inability to get an erection

insomnia: the inability to sleep

morning-after pill: emergency contraception that is taken soon after sexual intercourse in order to prevent pregnancy

labia majora: outer lips of the vulva

labia minora: inner lips of the vulva

oral sex: when a person's mouth or tongue is used to stimulate another person's genitalia

orgasm: the euphoric, emotional, and physical sensations that are felt at the end of sexual arousal when built-up muscle tension in the body is released; the climax of sensations that have been brought about by sexual excitement; the release of built-up muscle tension in the body that is a result of sexual arousal

ovulation: when a girl's body produces and releases an egg

perineum: area of skin between the vaginal opening and the anus in girls, and the scrotum and anus in guys

pre-ejaculate: the clear, slippery, and slightly thick fluid that comes out of a penis when a guy is sexually aroused

pre-pubescent: a person who has not started puberty

puberty: the physical transition of a child into an adult who is capable of reproduction

semen: ejaculate; cum

sexual orientation: what gender a person is attracted to

STD: sexually transmitted disease; any disease contracted through sexual intercourse or sexual contact

steroid: naturally or artificially created hormones

testes: plural of "testicle;" the part of the male genitalia that is commonly referred to as "the balls"

vagina: the moist canal in girls that leads from the uterus to the vulva

vibrator: a vibrating sex toy that is used for stimulation, often of the clitoris

virgin: a person who has never had sex

vulva: a girl's exterior genitalia; the full exterior anatomy of a girl

wet dream: an erotic dream that culminates in orgasm and ejaculation in guys

Index